EFFECTIVE COMMUNICATION SKILLS

Master the Art of Communication
and Unlock Your True Potential.

Ray Goodwin

CONTENTS

Title Page

Copyright

LIABILITY DISCLAIMER

Chapter 1: Introduction to Effective Communication   1

Chapter 2: Active Listening Skills   5

Chapter 3: Verbal Communication Skills   9

Chapter 4: Written Communication Skills   13

Chapter 5: Interpersonal Communication Skills   18

Chapter 6: Intercultural Communication Skills   21

Chapter 7: Group Communication Skills   25

Chapter 8: Leadership Communication Skills   29

Chapter 9: Business Communication Skills   33

Chapter 10: Family Communication Skills   38

Chapter 11: Classroom Communication Skills   43

Chapter 12: Health Communication Skills   47

Chapter 13: Media Communication Skills   52

Chapter 14: Public Speaking Skills   56

Chapter 15: Effective Communication in Romantic Relationships   60

Chapter 16: Effective Communication in Friendship   63

Chapter 17: Effective Communication at Work   67

Chapter 18: Effective Communication in Dating and Courtship 71

Chapter 19: Effective Communication in Parenting 74

Chapter 20: Effective Communication in Spiritual and Religious Settings 78

About The Author 83

LIABILITY DISCLAIMER

The information contained within this book is intended for informational purposes only and should not be construed as legal or professional advice. The authors and publishers of this book are not responsible for any losses or damages that may arise from the use of the information contained within.

The reader assumes full responsibility for any decisions made based on the information in this book. The authors and publishers do not endorse any particular method, service or product mentioned in this book and are not responsible for any consequences resulting from their use.

The reader should exercise caution and discretion when making life changing decisions, and should be aware of the risks and potential consequences of their actions. This book is not a substitute for professional or legal advice and should not be relied upon as such.

By reading and using the information in this book, the reader acknowledges and agrees to hold harmless the authors, publishers, and any other parties involved in the creation or distribution of this book from any and all liability, claims, damages, or losses that may arise from their use of the information contained herein.

CHAPTER 1: INTRODUCTION TO EFFECTIVE COMMUNICATION

Communication is an essential part of our daily lives. Whether it's at home, work, or in public, we are constantly communicating with those around us. However, communication doesn't always come naturally to everyone. Miscommunication can lead to misunderstandings and unnecessary conflicts.

Effective Communication Skills is a practical guidebook that provides readers with the tools they need to communicate effectively in any situation. The book covers a range of topics from body language and active listening to conflict resolution and public speaking.

As the author, I draw on my own experiences as a communications expert with over 25 years of experience in various industries including education, business, and government. I wrote this book because I believe that effective communication is not only important but also necessary for success.

Throughout the book, readers will learn how to identify barriers to effective communication and how to overcome them. They will also discover different techniques for delivering clear and concise messages that will help them achieve their goals.

Whether you're looking to improve your communication skills at work or in your personal life, Effective Communication Skills has everything you need to succeed.

Communication

Effective communication is the cornerstone of any successful relationship, whether it is personal or professional. Clear communication helps us to build trust, form meaningful connections, and achieve our goals. However, effective communication is more than just speaking clearly; it requires a deep understanding of the different types of communication, the elements that make it effective, and the common barriers that can prevent it.

So, what exactly is effective communication? At its core, effective communication is the ability to share information clearly and concisely, while remaining open to feedback and questions. It involves using listening skills, speaking clearly and confidently, and choosing the right mode of communication for a particular situation. It is the process of creating and maintaining relationships through open and honest dialogue.

There are many different types of communication, including verbal, nonverbal, written, and visual. Verbal communication includes words spoken aloud, while nonverbal communication encompasses body language, facial expressions, and tone of voice. Written communication involves any form of written text, from emails to reports. Visual communication includes any form of graphic or multimedia content, such as videos or infographics.

In order to achieve effective communication, there are several elements that must be in place. The first of these is clarity, meaning that the message being conveyed is easy to understand and articulate. The second is empathy, or the ability to understand and relate to the perspective of the person you are communicating with. The third is active listening, or the ability to pay attention and respond to what the other person is saying. Finally, effective communication requires congruence, or alignment between what you say and what you do.

However, there are also many common barriers that can prevent effective communication. These include physical barriers like distractions or noisy environments, emotional barriers like fear or anxiety, and cultural barriers like language or customs. Additionally, certain communication styles or personalities can make it difficult to connect with others.

Despite these obstacles, improving your communication skills can offer a wealth of benefits. Effective communication can improve your personal and professional relationships, enhance your leadership abilities, increase your productivity and efficiency, and help you to achieve your goals. The ability to communicate effectively is a valuable and highly sought-after skill in any industry or arena.

In this book, we will explore the many different aspects of effective communication. We will cover active listening skills, verbal communication skills, written communication skills, interpersonal communication skills, intercultural communication skills, group communication skills, leadership communication skills, business communication skills, family communication skills, classroom communication skills, health communication skills, media communication skills, public speaking skills, and effective communication in romantic relationships, friendships, dating and courtship, parenting, and spiritual and religious settings.

We will also discuss different strategies and exercises for improving your communication skills, setting communication goals, and overcoming common communication barriers. Whether you are a student, a professional, or just looking to strengthen your personal relationships, this book will give you the tools and techniques you need to communicate more effectively and build stronger connections with those around you.

CHAPTER 2: ACTIVE LISTENING SKILLS

Effective communication starts with active listening, which is the ability to give your full attention and understanding to the person who is speaking. In this chapter, we will discuss the importance of active listening, the techniques for active listening, and how to improve your listening skills.

What is active listening?

Active listening is more than just hearing what the other person is saying. It means engaging with the speaker, showing empathy and understanding, and responding appropriately. Active listening helps build trust and respect, and it is an essential skill for effective communication.

The importance of active listening

Active listening is crucial in improving communication because it helps you better understand the message being conveyed. It also shows the speaker that you value what they have to say and are interested in their thoughts and feelings. Additionally, it helps create a safe space for the speaker to share their ideas and express themselves, which is vital in relationships and professional settings.

Techniques for active listening

There are several techniques you can use when actively listening to someone, including:

❖ Eye contact: Making eye contact shows the speaker that you are interested in what they are saying and are present in the conversation.

❖ Nodding and verbal affirmations: Nodding and using phrases like "I understand" or "I see what you mean" demonstrate that you are following the conversation and help show the speaker that their thoughts and feelings are being heard.

❖ Paraphrasing: Paraphrasing involves restating the speaker's points in your own words to show that you understand their message and to clarify any potential misunderstandings.

❖ Asking open-ended questions: Asking questions that cannot be answered with a simple "yes" or "no" encourages the speaker to elaborate on their thoughts and feelings, thus providing more depth to the conversation.

Barriers to active listening

Several barriers can prevent active listening, including distractions, biases, and the urge to interrupt. Distractions can come from external sources, like noises in the background or a phone ringing, but they can also come from internal sources, like thinking about what you are going to say next. Biases can also interfere with active listening by causing preconceived notions about a person or situation.

The urge to interrupt can also be a barrier to active listening. Many people have a habit of interrupting someone mid-phrase or thought, which can be detrimental to effective communication. By interrupting, you may miss important information or cause the speaker to feel unimportant.

Listening skills exercises

There are several exercises you can try to improve your active listening skills. One simple exercise that involves a partner is the "mirror exercise." In this exercise, one partner describes a mundane object or experience to the other partner, who then repeats what they heard.

Another exercise is to listen to a podcast or TED talk and take notes on key points. After listening, discuss with a friend or colleague what you learned from the talk and the significance of the main points.

Understanding nonverbal communication

Nonverbal communication is the use of facial expressions, body language, and other nonverbal cues to convey a message. It is essential to understand nonverbal cues when actively listening. Some examples of nonverbal communication include eye contact, tone of voice, facial expressions, and body language.

Improving your listening skills

Improving your listening skills takes time and practice. Some tips to improve your listening skills are:

- ❖ Avoid distractions: When engaging in a conversation, avoid distractions like checking your phone or looking around the room.

- ❖ Focus on the speaker: Focus on the person speaking and make eye contact to show that you are engaged and listening.

- ❖ Ask clarifying questions: To show that you are actively listening, ask for clarification or more information.

- ❖ Avoid interrupting: Avoid interrupting the speaker mid-sentence and wait until they are finished speaking before responding.

Active listening in relationships

Active listening is critical in building and maintaining healthy relationships. By actively listening to your partner, you can strengthen your connection and intimacy. It also demonstrates that you value their thoughts and feelings, which can help build trust and respect.

Active listening can also help resolve conflicts in relationships. By actively listening to your partner's concerns and understanding their point of view, you can work towards a solution that benefits both parties.

In conclusion, active listening is an essential skill in effective communication because it helps build trust, respect, and understanding. It is a skill that takes time and practice to master, but it is critical in professional and personal settings. By using techniques like making eye contact, nodding and affirmations, paraphrasing, and asking open-ended questions, you can become a better active listener and improve your communication skills.

CHAPTER 3: VERBAL COMMUNICATION SKILLS

In this chapter, we explore the basics of verbal communication, including the role of language in communication, the power of words, and the impact of tone of voice. Effective speaking techniques and strategies for overcoming communication anxiety are also discussed.

The Role of Language in Communication

Language is the primary tool we use to communicate verbally. It is a system of words and symbols categorized by a set of grammatical rules that help to convey meaning clearly. Language is essential for effective communication, but language barriers can cause communication breakdowns, particularly in intercultural communication.

It is important to use clear and concise language when communicating, and to avoid using jargon or overly technical terms when communicating with people outside of your field. This can help to enhance understanding in the communication process.

The Power of Words

Words have the power to evoke emotions, create connections, and inspire change. They can also be used to denigrate, insult, or hurt others. As a result, it is important to choose your words carefully and use them sensitively in different contexts.

In business communication for example, using positive language can set the tone for productive conversations. Instead of saying, "This is a problem," you can say, "This is an opportunity for improvement." Using positive language can help to create a more favorable environment for effective communication.

The Impact of Tone of Voice

Tone of voice can have a significant impact on how a message is received. It determines the mood and attitude of the speaker and can reinforce or contradict the meaning of the words.

A speaker's tone can be perceived as aggressive, passive, or assertive. An aggressive tone can be perceived as hostile, while a passive tone can be perceived as submissive. An assertive tone, on the other hand, is confident, clear, and respectful of other people's perspectives.

Effective Speaking Techniques

To be an effective communicator, you need to be able to convey your message with skill and confidence. Here are some effective speaking techniques to help you achieve this:

❖ Speak clearly and with confidence - ensure that you speak loud enough to be heard, and enunciate your words clearly.

❖ Use appropriate body language - use body language that aligns with your words to reinforce your message.

❖ Pace your speech - speak at a pace that is easy to follow and allows your audience to process your message.

❖ Use pauses effectively - use pauses to allow for emphasis and to give your audience time to reflect on what you have said.

❖ Be mindful of your audience - adjust your tone, language, and pace to cater to your audience's needs and interests.

Overcoming Communication Anxiety

Many people struggle with anxiety when communicating, particularly when speaking in public or in important situations. However, by recognising the causes of communication anxiety and implementing strategies to address it, you can overcome it and improve your communication skills.

Some strategies you can use include preparing thoroughly before any important communication, practising your speaking skills, and reinterpreting negative expectations you have of yourself.

Public Speaking Tips

Public speaking can be especially daunting for many people. Here are some public speaking tips to help you communicate effectively:

❖ Prepare thoroughly - Research and prepare your speech well in advance, and practice it thoroughly.

❖ Start with a strong opening - Capture your audience's attention with a compelling opening statement or story.

❖ Structure your speech - Organize your speech into distinct sections with a clear beginning, middle, and end.

❖ Use visual aids - Use visual aids such as diagrams, slides and videos to help support and clarify your message.

❖ Engage your audience - Encourage audience participation through questions and interactive exercises.

❖ End with a clear call to action - End your speech with a call to action to inspire your audience to take action.

In summary, verbal communication is a vital tool in effective communication. It is a complex process that involves language, words, tone of voice, and effective use of speaking techniques. Overcoming communication anxiety and mastering public speaking skills are crucial for effective verbal communication. By paying attention to these elements and practicing effective communication techniques, you can become a confident and effective verbal communicator.

CHAPTER 4: WRITTEN COMMUNICATION SKILLS

In today's world, written communication has become an indispensable part of our personal and professional lives. Whether it's sending an email, writing a report, or creating a presentation, good writing skills are essential for clear and effective communication. In this chapter, we will explore the importance of written communication, its elements, and some tips and techniques to improve your writing skills.

The Importance of Written Communication

Written communication is important because it provides a documented record of ideas, thoughts, and actions. It also allows communication with people who are not physically present and serves as a useful tool for conveying complex information. In the business world, all official communication takes place in writing, and a poorly written message can lead to misunderstandings, delays, and even legal problems.

Elements of Effective Writing

Effective writing should be clear, concise, and organized. It should also be appropriate for the intended audience. Here are some key elements of effective writing:

➤ Clarity: The message should convey a clear meaning. Avoid using jargon, abbreviations, and technical terms that the reader may not be familiar with. Use simple sentences and avoid using too many words.

➤ Conciseness: Be brief and to the point. Avoid using unnecessary words and phrases that add no value to the message. Use the active voice, as it is more direct and easier to understand.

➤ Organization: The message should be well organized, with a clear beginning, middle and end. Use headings and subheadings to make the message easier to read and understand.

➤ Audience: Consider the intended audience and tailor the message to their needs. Use language that the audience will understand and avoid using industry jargon.

➤ Tone: The tone of the message should be appropriate for the context. Avoid using a tone that is too formal or too casual, and always maintain a professional tone.

Writing for Different Audiences

Writing for different audiences requires different approaches. For example, if you are writing for a technical audience, you may need to use technical jargon and be very specific. However, if you are writing for a general audience, you need to use simple language and avoid complicated terms.

Email Etiquette

Email is a popular and convenient means of communication, but it is important to use proper email etiquette. Here are some tips for writing effective emails:

➤ Use a clear subject line: The subject line should clearly

convey the purpose of the email.

➢ Keep it brief: Keep the email short and to the point.

➢ Be polite: Use polite language and avoid using all caps.

➢ Use proper grammar and spelling: Poor grammar and spelling can reflect badly on you and your organization.

➢ Use a professional salutation and closing: Use a professional opening and closing, such as "Dear Mr. Smith" and "Sincerely".

Professional Writing Tips

Here are some tips for writing professional documents, such as reports and proposals:

➢ Use a clear structure: Use headings, subheadings, and bullet points to make the document easier to read and understand.

➢ Use proper formatting: Use a professional font, such as Times New Roman or Arial, and use proper spacing and margins.

➢ Use graphics and visual aids: Use charts, graphs, and images to make the document more engaging and understandable.

➢ Revise and edit: Proofread the document carefully for errors and revise, as necessary.

Writing Reports and Proposals

In the business world, reports and proposals are an important means of communication. Here are some tips for writing effective reports and proposals:

➢ Understand the purpose: Understand the purpose of the report or proposal and tailor the message accordingly.

> Use a clear structure: Use headings, subheadings, and bullet points to make the document easy to read and understand.

> Use evidence: Use evidence to support your arguments and conclusions.

> Be concise: Be brief and to the point.

> Include recommendations: Make recommendations based on your analysis and conclusions.

Proofreading and Editing Techniques

Proofreading and editing are important to ensure that your written communication is clear and error-free. Here are some tips for proofreading and editing:

> Take a break: Take a break before proofreading to clear your mind.

> Read out loud: Reading out loud can help you catch errors and improve flow.

> Use online tools: Use online tools, such as Grammarly or Hemingway, to help identify errors.

> Focus on one issue at a time: Focus on one issue at a time, such as grammar or spelling, to make sure you catch all the errors.

Social Media Writing Guidelines

Social media has become an important means of communication, but it is important to use proper social media writing guidelines. Here are some tips for writing effective social media posts:

> Understand the platform: Understand the platform and tailor the message accordingly.

> Use a clear structure: Use short paragraphs and bullet

points to make the message easy to read and understand.

> Use visuals: Use images and videos to make the post more engaging.

> Be concise: Keep the post short and to the point.

> Use hashtags: Use hashtags to make the post more discoverable.

In conclusion, effective written communication is essential for personal and professional success. By following some simple tips and techniques, you can improve your writing skills and communicate more effectively. Remember to tailor your writing to the intended audience and use proper etiquette in all your communication.

CHAPTER 5: INTERPERSONAL COMMUNICATION SKILLS

Interpersonal communication is the essence of human interaction, and it involves exchanging ideas, feelings, and information with another person or group of people. For successful interactions, it is crucial to hone interpersonal communication skills. This chapter takes an in-depth look at interpersonal communication skills.

What is Interpersonal Communication?

Interpersonal communication is the exchange of information, feelings, and ideas between two or more people. It involves both verbal and nonverbal communication, and it can take place in a variety of settings, such as personal relationships, work settings, and social gatherings.

The Importance of Interpersonal Communication

Effective interpersonal communication is the cornerstone of successful relationships and collaborations. The way we communicate with others can impact our personal and professional lives. Clear communication is essential for establishing trust, understanding, and mutual respect.

Building Rapport

Building rapport is about creating a connection with another person. It is the process of establishing mutual trust, understanding, and respect. To build rapport, it is essential to listen actively, show genuine interest, and find common ground.

Conflict Resolution Techniques

Conflict is an inevitable part of human interaction, and it can lead to stress, frustration, and misunderstandings. However, conflict can also be an opportunity to build stronger relationships and improve communication skills. Effective conflict resolution involves active listening, empathy, and finding win-win solutions that address the underlying issues.

Assertiveness vs. Aggressiveness

Assertiveness is about expressing your needs, wants, and feelings in a clear and direct manner, while respecting the needs and boundaries of others. Aggressiveness, on the other hand, involves forcing your opinions or desires on others without regard for their feelings or needs. To be assertive, it is crucial to understand your rights, communicate clearly, and seek compromises.

Negotiation Skills

Negotiation is the process of finding a mutually acceptable solution to a problem, and it is a critical interpersonal communication skill. Effective negotiation involves active listening, asking questions, and being willing to compromise.

Emotional Intelligence

Emotional intelligence is the ability to recognize, understand, and manage your own emotions, as well as the emotions of others. It is an essential interpersonal communication skill, as it helps individuals establish healthy relationships, communicate more effectively, and handle conflicts respectfully.

Developing Empathy

Empathy involves understanding and sharing the feelings of others. It is an essential interpersonal skill, as it helps individuals build rapport, communicate effectively, and resolve conflicts. Empathy requires active listening, seeking to understand others' perspectives, and showing genuine concern for their feelings.

In conclusion, honing interpersonal communication skills is essential for establishing and maintaining healthy relationships both personally and professionally. By building rapport, resolving conflicts, being assertive, negotiating effectively, developing emotional intelligence, and empathy, one can develop strong interpersonal communication skills.

CHAPTER 6: INTERCULTURAL COMMUNICATION SKILLS

Effective communication is an essential aspect of any successful relationship, whether personal or professional. However, when attempting to communicate with someone from a different cultural background, it becomes significantly more challenging to achieve effective communication. This is where the concept of intercultural communication comes into play.

Defining Intercultural Communication

Intercultural communication can be defined as communication between individuals or groups from different cultures. It involves understanding and respecting cultural differences that can impact communication, such as language barriers, societal norms, and cultural values. Understanding and properly navigating these differences can lead to more effective communication and better relationships between individuals and groups from different backgrounds.

Understanding Cultural Differences

To effectively communicate with someone from a different

cultural background, it's essential to first understand and respect their cultural differences. These differences can be subtle or significant, and failing to acknowledge and respect them can lead to misunderstandings and conflicts.

One critical aspect of culture is language. Even if two individuals speak the same language, there can still be differences in dialects, slang, and other language nuances that can impact communication. It's crucial to be patient in conversations and ask for clarification when necessary.

Societal norms can also differ significantly across cultures. For example, in some cultures, it's considered impolite to be direct or assertive in communication, while in others, it's expected. Understanding these cultural norms and adapting communication styles accordingly can make a significant difference in achieving effective communication.

Cultural Barriers to Effective Communication

Some of the most significant barriers to effective intercultural communication are language barriers, stereotypes, and cultural differences in communication styles.

Language barriers can be challenging to overcome, especially if both parties don't speak each other's language. However, there are ways to mitigate these barriers, such as using translation tools or hiring interpreters.

Stereotypes can also significantly impact communication between individuals from different cultures. Preconceived notions about certain cultures can lead to bias and insensitivity, which can make it challenging to establish trust and respect.

Finally, cultural differences in communication styles can present a significant barrier to effective communication. For example, some cultures might consider it rude to interrupt a speaker, while others might consider it perfectly acceptable. Understanding and adapting to these cultural differences can significantly improve the chances of effective communication.

Developing Cultural Sensitivity

Developing cultural sensitivity is essential when attempting to communicate with individuals from different backgrounds. It involves being aware and respectful of cultural differences and avoiding behaviors or language that could be considered insensitive or offensive.

Developing cultural sensitivity requires a willingness to learn about other cultures actively. It involves asking questions, seeking understanding, and avoiding assumptions. It also requires acknowledging and apologizing for any mistakes made due to cultural misunderstandings.

Nonverbal Communication Across Cultures

Nonverbal communication can differ significantly across cultures and can impact how an individual is perceived. For example, in some cultures, making direct eye contact is considered a sign of respect, while in others, it's inappropriate.

To avoid misunderstandings in nonverbal communication, it's important to be aware of cultural differences. This involves understanding the subtle nuances in body language, gestures, and facial expressions that may differ across cultures.

Building Cross-Cultural Relationships

Building cross-cultural relationships can be challenging, but it's essential for effective intercultural communication. It involves being patient, respectful, and willing to learn about other cultures actively.

One critical aspect of building cross-cultural relationships is establishing trust and respect. This can be achieved by demonstrating sincerity, empathy, and cultural sensitivity in communication. It's also essential to be open-minded and avoid making assumptions or generalizations about other cultures.

Strategies for Avoiding Misunderstandings

To avoid misunderstandings in intercultural communication, it's crucial to be aware of cultural differences and avoid making assumptions or generalizations about other cultures. One strategy is to ask clarifying questions and seek to understand before communicating.

Another strategy is to avoid the use of slang or idioms, which can be easily misinterpreted by individuals who don't speak the same language. Being clear and concise in communication and using simple language can also help avoid misunderstandings.

Successful Communication in a Globalized World

In a globalized world, effective intercultural communication is essential for building relationships, achieving business success, and promoting cultural understanding. By understanding and respecting cultural differences, developing cultural sensitivity, and communicating clearly and effectively, individuals and groups from different backgrounds can communicate successfully and build strong, lasting relationships.

CHAPTER 7: GROUP COMMUNICATION SKILLS

Communication is an essential part of any working environment. However, when it comes to working collaboratively in groups, communication can become more complex and challenging. Group communication has become increasingly relevant in today's work culture. This chapter will discuss the nature of group communication, effective teamwork, building trust and collaboration, managing conflict in groups, meeting facilitation skills, virtual group communication, and giving and receiving feedback.

The Nature of Group Communication

Group communication is the exchange of information between two or more people, working together to achieve a common goal. Effective group communication is essential for the success of any business or organization. The key characteristic of group communication is the presence of multiple participants working towards a common objective. Group communication is different from individual communication, as it involves more social processes and interdependence between members of the group.

Effective Teamwork

Effective teamwork is a critical component of group communication. A team refers to a group of individuals working together towards a common goal. Effective teamwork is vital for the success of any project and can make all the difference between success and failure. To achieve effective teamwork, group members must work collaboratively towards a common goal, communicate transparently, share knowledge and expertise, and respect one another. A team's success depends on the ability to collaborate and build productive relationships.

Building Trust and Collaboration

Trust is fundamental to successful group communication. When group members trust one another, they can work effectively towards a common goal. Trust can be built by fostering open communication, sharing knowledge and expertise, and demonstrating transparency. Collaboration is another critical component of group communication. Collaboration involves a group working together to achieve a common goal, leveraging the strengths and expertise of each member. Teams that collaborate effectively have strong relationships and are better equipped to handle challenges and conflicts that arise.

Managing Conflict in Groups

Conflict is inevitable in any working environment, and group communication is no exception. It is essential to deal with conflicts effectively to maintain the group's productivity and cohesion. The key to managing conflict in groups involves identifying the source of the conflict, actively listening to the points of views of others, and finding a common ground for resolution. It is crucial to understand that conflict can be constructive, leading to new insights and ideas. However, if not managed correctly, conflict can lead to tension, misunderstandings, and resentment.

Meeting Facilitation Skills

Effective meeting facilitation is a vital component of group communication. A facilitator's role is to help the group work together effectively towards a common goal while ensuring that all group members' voices are heard. A facilitator should be able to manage conflicts, build consensus, and extract ideas from every member of the group. An effective meeting facilitator should have excellent communication skills, be able to manage group dynamics, and be organized in coordinating meeting arrangements.

Virtual Group Communication

Virtual group communication refers to communication that occurs online, primarily through video conferencing tools like Zoom or Skype. Virtual group communication has gained a lot of popularity in recent years, primarily due to the increase in remote working. However, virtual group communication can be challenging due to technical issues, time zone differences, and lack of physical presence. To succeed in virtual group communication, it is essential to establish clear communication protocols, use technology effectively, and establish rapport among group members.

Giving and Receiving Feedback

Feedback is a crucial component of group communication. Feedback can help individuals improve their work, learn from their mistakes, and achieve their goals. Giving feedback involves offering constructive criticism in a way that is respectful and helpful, whereas receiving feedback involves being open to suggestions for improvement. Effective feedback should be specific, objective, timely, and relevant. It is essential to establish a culture of feedback within the group to ensure that everyone feels comfortable providing and receiving feedback.

Conclusion

Group communication is essential for the success of any business or organization. Effective communication within a group allows for collaboration, transparency, and the development of strong relationships. Effective teamwork, building trust and collaboration, managing conflict in groups, meeting facilitation skills, virtual group communication, and giving and receiving feedback are all critical components of group communication. In a group setting, it is important to remember that each member has a unique perspective to bring, and each member's opinion should be respected and heard. By effectively communicating within a group, individuals can work collaboratively towards their goals, leading to success for everyone involved.

CHAPTER 8: LEADERSHIP COMMUNICATION SKILLS

As a leader, effective communication skills are essential in order to be successful. Without the ability to communicate effectively, your team may struggle to understand your vision and goals for the business, leading to a lack of motivation and productivity. It is also important to communicate in a way that builds trust and credibility amongst your team and stakeholders. In this chapter, we will explore the key elements of leadership communication and provide strategies for effective communication.

The Role of Communication in Leadership

Communication is a foundational element of leadership, as it drives the vision and direction of the business. As a leader, you must be able to clearly articulate your goals and expectations to your team, as well as communicate effectively with other stakeholders such as customers, suppliers, and investors. Effective communication provides clarity, ensures that everyone is working towards the same objectives, and promotes accountability and responsibility.

The Importance of Clear Vision and Values

Creating a clear vision and set of values for your business is crucial, as it provides the foundation for your leadership communication. Your vision and values should reflect what your business stands for, where it is headed, and how it will get there. Communicating your vision and values in a clear and consistent manner ensures that everyone within the business can align their actions with the overarching purpose of the business.

Communicating with Authority

A key aspect of leadership communication is the ability to communicate with authority. This means speaking confidently, clearly, and assertively. When you communicate with authority, others will be more likely to listen and respect your message. It is important to strike a balance between being assertive and being aggressive, as overly aggressive communication can undermine your credibility and damage relationships.

Building Credibility and Trust

Credibility and trust are essential components of leadership communication, as they are the foundation upon which relationships are built. To build credibility and trust, it is important to be consistent in your messaging, follow through on commitments, and demonstrate your expertise and knowledge. Transparency and authenticity are also important, as they allow others to see that you are a trustworthy and reliable leader.

Motivating and Inspiring Others

Effective leadership communication is not just about transmitting information, it is also about inspiring and motivating others. As a leader, it is your job to create a sense of purpose and direction for your team, and to help them see how their work fits into the bigger picture. This requires communication that is both inspiring and practical, providing clarity around goals and objectives, while engaging hearts and minds.

Effective Delegation

Delegation is an essential leadership function, and clear communication is key to successful delegation. When delegating tasks to others, it is important to clearly communicate expectations, goals, and timelines, ensuring that everyone is on the same page. This can involve providing clear instructions, setting performance standards, and offering feedback on progress.

Handling Difficult Conversations

Leadership also involves handling difficult conversations, such as performance reviews, conflicts, and disciplinary actions. These conversations require powerful communication skills, as they often involve high emotions and sensitive issues. Effective communication in these situations requires careful preparation, sensitivity, and the ability to listen actively and respond with empathy.

Leading Through Change

Finally, leadership communication is critical when leading through change. Change can be disruptive and uncomfortable, which can lead to resistance and confusion amongst team members. Effective communication is key to navigating change successfully, as it can help to create a sense of urgency, clarify expectations, and provide guidance on what actions need to be taken.

Conclusion

Effective communication skills are essential for leadership

success, providing the foundation upon which relationships, motivation, and productivity are built. Whether you are communicating your vision and values, delegating tasks, handling difficult conversations, or leading through change, clarity, consistency, and authenticity are key. By mastering leadership communication skills, you can foster a positive and productive organizational environment, inspiring and motivating your team to achieve their goals.

CHAPTER 9: BUSINESS COMMUNICATION SKILLS

Effective communication is crucial in the business world. The way you communicate can impact how you are perceived, how you build relationships, how you negotiate deals, and how successful you are in achieving your goals. This chapter will cover the role of communication in business, important business communication techniques, and strategies for successfully communicating in different business scenarios.

Professionalism in Communication

Effective business communication starts with professionalism. Having a professional demeanor and using proper language and tone can help build credibility and trust with clients, colleagues, and other business partners. One way to maintain professionalism is by using appropriate greetings and salutations in your email communications. For example, when addressing a business client, you might start your email with "Dear Mr./Ms. Last Name" followed by a professional greeting such as "I hope this email finds you well." Avoid using casual language or slang, even if you are communicating with colleagues who are also friends.

Another important element of professionalism in business communication is tone. The tone of your message can impact how it is received by the person on the receiving end. Be mindful of your tone and try to keep it positive and respectful, even when addressing difficult or sensitive topics. If you are communicating bad news or criticism, it is important to be compassionate and direct without being disrespectful or condescending.

Business Writing Techniques

In the business world, effective communication often requires strong writing skills. This includes writing emails, business proposals, and reports, as well as other types of professional writing. Business writing should be clear and concise, addressing the main point quickly and using appropriate language.

When writing emails, use bullet points or clear paragraph breaks to organize your thoughts and make the email easy to read. Keep the tone friendly and positive, but avoid using unnecessary pleasantries that can dilute your message. Use simple, direct language and avoid jargon or technical language that the recipient might not understand.

When crafting business proposals or reports, it is important to be thorough and professional. Use a clear and organized structure, with headings and subheadings to guide the reader through the document. Use charts or diagrams to illustrate key points and support your argument. Avoid lengthy paragraphs or excessive use of technical language, which can be overwhelming and hard to follow.

Crafting Effective Presentations

Effective presentations can be a powerful tool for winning business, closing a deal, or convincing your audience of your message. A successful presentation requires both strong content and effective delivery.

When creating a presentation, start with a clear outline that includes the main points you want to cover and the order in which you want to present them. Slides should be visually appealing but not too cluttered, with clear, concise information. Use graphics or diagrams to illustrate key points and make the presentation more engaging.

When delivering a presentation, body language and tone of voice are just as important as the content. Speak clearly and confidently, making eye contact with your audience. Use hand gestures and other body language to emphasize key points and maintain engagement. Be mindful of your pace - speaking too quickly can make it hard for your audience to keep up, while speaking too slowly can make it boring and difficult to follow.

Sales and Negotiation Skills

Effective communication is key to success in sales and negotiation. When selling a product or service, it is important to understand the customer's needs and communicate how your offering can address those needs. Listen carefully to their concerns and tailor your message accordingly. Provide evidence or case studies to support your claims and build credibility.

In a negotiation, effective communication means being able to clearly articulate your position and understand the position of the other party. Use active listening skills and ask questions to understand their needs and priorities. Seek common ground and aim for a mutually beneficial outcome. Avoid confrontational language or tactics, which can quickly escalate the situation and damage the relationship.

Customer Service Communication

Customers are the lifeblood of any business, and effective communication is key to providing exceptional customer service. This includes listening carefully to customer complaints or concerns, responding in a timely manner, and offering solutions that meet their needs.

When dealing with difficult or unhappy customers, it is important to remain calm and approach the situation with empathy. Use active listening skills to understand their concerns and offer solutions that address those concerns. Be patient and respectful, even if the customer is angry or upset. A successful resolution can often turn an unhappy customer into a loyal one.

Project Management Communication

Effective communication is essential in project management, where multiple stakeholders and team members must work together to achieve a common goal. Clear communication of project goals and objectives is important from the outset, as is keeping stakeholders informed of progress throughout the project.

Use regular project meetings and status updates to ensure that team members are up-to-date on project progress, milestones, and deadlines. When delegating tasks, be clear on expectations and timelines. Use collaborative tools such as project management software or team collaboration tools to facilitate communication and coordination. Be open to feedback and adjust the project plan as needed to ensure that goals are met, and stakeholders are satisfied.

Social Media and Branding

Social media plays an increasingly important role in business communication, offering a powerful platform for building brand awareness and engagement with customers. Effective social media communication requires a clear understanding of your brand voice and message, as well as the needs and preferences of your target audience.

When using social media for business, use a consistent brand voice and message across all channels. Engage with your audience through comments, direct messages, and other interactions. Make use of visual elements such as images or videos to help your message stand out. Finally, be mindful of online communication etiquette, avoiding negative or controversial comments that could bring negative attention to your brand.

Conclusion

Effective communication is a critical component of success in the business world. By maintaining professionalism in communication, using strong writing and presentation skills, and effectively interacting with customers, colleagues, and other stakeholders, you can build strong relationships and achieve your goals. With the right strategies and techniques, you can successfully navigate different communication scenarios and achieve success in your business endeavors.

CHAPTER 10: FAMILY COMMUNICATION SKILLS

Family communication is one of the most crucial aspects that shapes the relationships within the family. It is the medium through which family members exchange ideas, thoughts, opinions, emotions, and information. Open and effective family communication can lead to a better understanding of each other, reduce conflicts, and strengthen the family bonds.

Types of Family Communication

The communication within a family can be broadly categorized into four types:

➢ Open Communication: Here, the family members openly share their feelings, thoughts, and opinions without any fear of judgment or criticism.

➢ Closed Communication: In this type of communication, there is a lack of trust and understanding among family members. They do not express their feelings openly and may even withhold information from each other.

➢ Aggressive Communication: This type of communication involves the use of hurtful language, shouting and yelling, threatening, or demeaning behavior to express one's opinions or feelings.

➤ Passive Communication: This type of communication involves hiding one's emotions or opinions in the belief that it is safer or more comfortable not to express them.

Communication Patterns and Styles

Understanding the communication patterns and styles of the family members is crucial in improving family communication. The following are the patterns and styles of communication:

➤ Listening: Active listening is essential in effective family communication. Each family member must actively listen to others, understand their perspectives, and empathize with them.

➤ Nonverbal communication: Body language, facial expressions, and tone of voice can convey emotions and feelings more effectively than words. Understanding nonverbal cues can help in understanding the deeper meaning behind the words.

➤ Assertiveness: Assertive communication involves expressing opinions, feelings, and beliefs in a clear, concise, and respectful manner, without attacking or belittling others.

➤ Empathy: Understanding and acknowledging the feelings and perspectives of others is essential in developing healthy communication within families. Empathy helps reduce conflicts and fosters a sense of emotional connectedness.

Overcoming Family Communication Barriers

Common barriers to effective family communication include:

➤ Lack of time: Busy schedules and conflicting priorities can reduce the time available for family communication.

➤ Differences in communication styles: Different

family members may have different communication styles, making it difficult to communicate effectively.

➢   Emotional barriers: Negative emotions such as anger, fear, and resentment can hinder effective communication, leading to misunderstandings and conflicts.

➢   Generational gaps: Differences in age and life experiences between family members can lead to communication barriers.

To overcome these barriers, identifying the root cause of communication issues, actively listening to each other, expressing emotions and feelings honestly, showing empathy and compassion, and practicing assertive communication can help improve family communication.

Building Healthy Relationships

Effective family communication plays a significant role in building healthy relationships within the family. The following techniques can help in building stronger family relationships:

➢   Building trust: Trust is crucial in any relationship. Ensuring that the family members keep their promises, maintaining confidentiality, avoiding dishonesty, and being transparent can communicate trustworthiness.

➢   Expressing affection: Expressing love and affection can foster a sense of comfort and security among family members.

➢   Recognizing individual differences: Understand that every family member is unique, with their set of emotions, thoughts, and beliefs. Recognizing and respecting these differences can promote mutual understanding and build stronger relationships.

Parent-Child Communication

Parent-child communication is one of the most critical forms of communication within the family. Effective parent-child communication involves:

➢ Active listening: Children want their parents to listen to them and empathize with their problems and emotions. Parents should ensure they maintain eye contact and show interest in what their children are saying.

➢ Age-appropriate communication: It is essential to communicate with children based on their age and developmental stage. Communicating at their level of comprehension can help maintain their interest and actively engage them.

➢ Being a positive role model: Children learn by observing their role models. Parents should be a role model for the behavior they want their children to emulate.

Sibling Communication

Sibling communication can be complicated due to the different personalities, interests, and age differences. The following techniques can help in building stronger sibling relationships:

➢ Respect individual differences: Siblings should respect each other's unique characteristics and personality traits.

➢ Communicate openly and honestly: Encourage siblings to express their opinions and feelings. Encouraging active listening can help build stronger relationships.

➢ Resolve conflicts: Conflicts between siblings are inevitable, but discussing them and finding a resolution can help strengthen the sibling bond.

Conflict Resolution in Families

Effective conflict resolution is crucial in every family. Establishing conflict resolution rules, such as staying calm, actively listening, expressing emotions clearly, and proposing solutions, can help reduce conflicts and build stronger family relationships.

Conclusion

Effective family communication is crucial in building healthy and strong family relationships. It requires active listening, empathy, respect, and open and honest communication. Overcoming communication barriers, recognizing individual differences, and resolving conflicts are vital techniques for successful family communication. Parents and siblings who practice effective communication can improve their relationships and strengthen the family bond.

CHAPTER 11: CLASSROOM COMMUNICATION SKILLS

Effective communication is paramount in any setting, and it is crucial in the classroom setting. The importance of communication in education cannot be overemphasized as it leads to a better relationship between the students and the teachers, creating an enabling environment for learning. Effective communication in the classroom involves listening, understanding, and communicating with students, fellow teachers, and parents/guardians. The following are some of the tips for effective communication in the classroom.

Teacher-student communication

The teacher-student relationship is one of the most important relationships in the classroom setting. The teacher should strive to create a comfortable teaching and learning environment by having open communication with students. The communication should be respectful, engaging, and free of any form of antagonism. The teacher should also seek to understand the communication style of each student to foster a better understanding. The communication should take into consideration that different students learn differently and it is the teacher's duty to adjust his or her teaching style accordingly.

Effective classroom management

Effective classroom management is key to creating an enabling learning environment. It is important to have clear expectations, guidelines and rules that are communicated to the students. The teacher should make an effort to create an environment that is engaging, supportive, and conducive to learning. The teacher should seek to understand the unique qualities of each student, the different learning styles, and tailor his or her teaching style accordingly. The teacher should also establish an open line of communication with the students to be able to identify and address any emerging concerns.

Engaging and interactive teaching

Effective communication in the classroom should involve interactive teaching methods that stimulate and engage the students. The teacher can create a good learning environment by mixing teaching methods thus catering to students with different learning styles. The teacher can use visual aids, audio aids, group work, discussions, and other interactive methods that help to create an environment that is conducive to learning.

Building relationships with students

The teacher should strive to build open and honest relationships with the students. The communication should be respectful, supportive, and free from any form of antagonism. The teacher should seek to understand the issues that each student is facing, and use that understanding to help create a more conducive learning environment. The teacher should take an interest in the lives of the students, be approachable, and have an open door policy. This creates a nurturing environment that helps the students feel safe and comfortable, and in turn helps to create a better classroom learning experience.

Effective feedback and assessment

Effective communication in the classroom requires timely and constructive feedback. Giving feedback is an essential part of the learning process as it helps the student to identify their strengths and weaknesses. The teacher should create an environment where the students feel comfortable enough to ask questions or seek clarification. The teacher should give feedback that is respectful, constructive, and in a timely manner. The feedback should also take into consideration the different learning styles of the students.

Communication with parents/guardians

Effective communication with parents/guardians is crucial as it helps to keep the parents/guardians up-to-date with the happenings in the classroom. Regular communication updates create a sense of involvement and participation in the learning process. The teacher should create an environment where the parents/guardians feel comfortable enough to ask questions or seek clarification. Clear communication channels should be established that allows for feedback and constructive criticism.

Inclusive and diverse classroom communication

Inclusive and diverse communication fosters a learning environment that is enriched with diversity. It is important to recognize and acknowledge the diversity in the classroom and ensure that the communication is inclusive of all the students. It is important to understand the different cultural and language differences and tailoring the communication style to accommodate these differences. The teacher should seek to understand the different backgrounds and create an environment that is comfortable for all the students. Inclusivity not only helps students to feel included, but it also helps to foster a sense of understanding and respect for other cultures.

Conclusion

Effective communication is essential in the classroom as it is in every other area of life. The teacher should strive to create an environment that is nurturing, respectful, and engaging. The teacher should tailor the teaching style to cater to the different learning styles of the students and use interactive teaching methods to create an environment that is conducive to learning. Effective feedback and assessment, as well as inclusive and diverse communication, helps to create a learning environment that is enriched with diversity. In conclusion, effective communication in the classroom is essential in creating an environment that is conducive to learning and fosters open and honest communication.

CHAPTER 12: HEALTH COMMUNICATION SKILLS

Effective health communication is essential for ensuring that individuals have access to accurate, reliable, and understandable information that empowers them to make informed decisions about their health and well-being. Health communication occurs in many forms, including conversations between healthcare professionals and their patients, health promotion campaigns, and digital communication such as social media and mobile applications. Developing effective health communication skills is necessary for promoting healthy behaviors, building trust between providers and patients, and reducing health disparities.

Understanding Health Literacy

Health literacy is the ability to understand and use health information to make informed decisions about one's health. Low health literacy has been linked to poor health outcomes, increased healthcare utilization, and higher healthcare costs. It is estimated that nearly 90 million adults in the United States have low health literacy. To ensure that patients have the information they need to make informed decisions about their health, healthcare professionals should take steps to improve health literacy.

One approach to improving health literacy is to use plain language when communicating with patients. This means using simple words and avoiding jargon, technical language, and acronyms that patients may not understand. Providers should also use visuals, such as diagrams and pictures, to help patients understand complex medical concepts. Additionally, providers should take the time to ensure that patients have understood the information provided to them by asking follow-up questions and summarizing the information discussed.

Patient-Provider Communication

Effective patient-provider communication is essential for building trust and promoting patient-centered care. Effective communication involves listening to patients' concerns, providing clear explanations of medical conditions and treatment options, and ensuring that patients have the information they need to make informed decisions about their health.

To build effective patient-provider communication, providers should take the time to establish rapport with their patients by asking open-ended questions, actively listening to their responses, and acknowledging their concerns. Providers should also take the time to explain medical conditions and treatment options in plain language, using visuals when appropriate. Patients should be encouraged to ask questions and to express their concerns to their provider.

Communicating About Sensitive Health Topics

Health communication involves discussing sensitive topics such as sexual health, mental health, and substance use. Effective communication requires sensitivity, empathy, and respect for patients' feelings and concerns.

To communicate effectively about sensitive health topics, healthcare providers should create a safe and supportive environment that allows patients to discuss their concerns without fear of judgment or stigma. Providers should use nonjudgmental language, and should ask open-ended questions that encourage patients to share their experiences. Additionally, providers should be aware of cultural beliefs and practices that may impact patients' health behaviors and should take these into account when developing health promotion strategies.

Health Promotion Communication

Health promotion communication involves using communication strategies to promote healthy behaviors and to encourage patients to adopt healthy lifestyles. Effective health promotion communication should be tailored to the needs of the audience and should be based on sound health promotion principles.

One way to develop effective health promotion communication is to use social marketing principles. Social marketing involves using marketing techniques to promote healthy behaviors. Social marketing campaigns should be based on a thorough understanding of the target audience and should use messages and visuals that resonate with the audience. Additionally, social marketing campaigns should include calls to action that encourage individuals to adopt healthy behaviors.

Communicating in Crisis Situations

Effective communication is critical in crisis situations such as natural disasters or disease outbreaks. During these situations, it is important to provide accurate and timely information to the public to ensure that individuals can protect themselves and their families.

To communicate effectively during crisis situations, communication plans should be in place that allow for rapid dissemination of information. Communication plans should be developed in advance and should include strategies for communicating via multiple channels, such as social media, television, and radio. Additionally, communication plans should be based on the principles of risk communication, which involves providing clear and accurate information that acknowledges uncertainty and that provides actionable guidance to the public.

Health Communication Technologies

Health communication technologies, such as mobile applications and social media, offer new opportunities for promoting healthy behaviors and providing health information to the public. These technologies can be used to reach large audiences rapidly and to increase access to health information.

To use health communication technologies effectively, it is important to be aware of the strengths and limitations of each technology. For example, mobile applications can be used to provide individuals with personalized health information and reminders, while social media can be used to engage large audiences and to promote health initiatives. Additionally, it is important to ensure that health information provided through these technologies is accurate and reliable.

Ethical Considerations in Health Communication

Health communication raises a number of ethical considerations, such as privacy, autonomy, and informed consent. Healthcare providers must be aware of these ethical considerations and must take steps to ensure that they are adhering to ethical standards in their communication with patients.

One way to ensure ethical communication is to obtain informed consent from patients before sharing their health information with others. Additionally, providers should take steps to protect the privacy of patients, such as using secure communication channels and ensuring that patient information is not shared unnecessarily. Finally, providers should ensure that they are providing patients with accurate and reliable health information and should avoid using scare tactics or other unethical communication strategies.

Conclusion

Effective health communication is a critical component of promoting healthy behaviors, building trust between providers and patients, and reducing health disparities. Developing effective health communication skills requires a sensitivity to patients' needs and concerns, the ability to listen actively and communicate clearly, and an understanding of the ethical considerations that arise in healthcare communication. By developing effective health communication skills, healthcare providers can promote the health and well-being of their patients and improve the healthcare system as a whole.

CHAPTER 13: MEDIA COMMUNICATION SKILLS

Media communication has a powerful impact on individuals and society. When messages are communicated effectively through various media channels, they have the potential to bring about social change, raise awareness, and motivate action. In this chapter, we will explore the role of media in communication, the different types of media channels, and strategies for crafting effective media messages.

The role of media in communication:

Media plays a critical role in shaping our perceptions and attitudes. It has the power to influence how we think, feel, and act, often shaping our understanding of reality. Media channels include all forms of mass communication, including television, radio, newspapers, magazines, advertising, social media, and more.

With the rise of the internet, it has become increasingly easier for people to access and consume media content. This has led to digital media becoming a popular communication tool among individuals and organizations.

Understanding media audiences:

To create effective media messages, it is essential to understand the target audience. Without understanding the audience, media communication is likely to be less effective and may fail to achieve its goals. When creating media messages, it is important to consider factors such as age, gender, socio-economic status, cultural background, education level, and values.

Crafting effective media messages:

Effective media communication starts with a clear message that resonates with the target audience. Messages should be well-crafted to ensure they are memorable, engaging, and impactful. Here are some tips for crafting effective media messages:

- ➢ Start with a clear objective: Before creating media messages, start by defining the objective of the communication. What do you want to achieve? Do you want to raise awareness, educate, or motivate action?

- ➢ Understand the target audience: As mentioned earlier, it is critical to understand the target audience. What do they care about? What are their values? What motivates them?

- ➢ Choose the right media channel: Different media channels have different strengths and weaknesses. Choose the right channel to reach your target audience effectively.

- ➢ Keep it simple: Avoid complexity in media messages. Keep the message simple and easy to understand.

- ➢ Make it memorable: Use language that is catchy and memorable. Use visuals, such as images or videos, to enhance the message.

Media relations and public relations:

Media relations and public relations are crucial skills required for effective communication with media channels. These skills enable individuals and organizations to gain media exposure, reach a broader audience and communicate their message effectively.

Media relations are about building relationships with media channels and reporters. Effective media relations depend on trust, credibility, and the ability to provide reliable and accurate information. Public relations, on the other hand, are about promoting an organization or individual to the general public through various communication channels. Good public relations depend on developing a positive image through effective communication strategies.

Crisis communication in media:

Organizations may face a crisis that requires effective communication with the media. During a crisis, it is crucial to communicate quickly, accurately, and consistently. A well-crafted crisis communication plan can help organizations to manage crises and maintain their reputation.

Ethics in media communication:

Ethics plays a crucial role in media communication. Ethical communication means adhering to the principles of honesty, transparency, and respect for the audience. Ethics in media communication require adhering to the highest professional standards, including clarity, accuracy, and objectivity.

Social media and digital communication:

Social media has become an increasingly popular tool for media communication in recent years. Social media offers many opportunities to reach a broader audience, communicate messages effectively, and engage with viewers.

However, social media also poses many challenges due to its fast-paced nature and the need to keep up with emerging trends. To succeed in social media, it is important to develop a strong social media strategy, identify the right platforms, and produce content that is both engaging and informative.

Media communication for social change:

Media communication can play a vital role in promoting social change. However, to achieve social change, media messages must be compelling and targeted towards the right audience.

Effective media communication for social change requires creating strong, persuasive messages that inspire people to take action. A strong message can be a powerful catalyst for change, driving people to take action both individually and collectively.

Conclusion:

Media communication can be a powerful tool for communication. However, it requires careful crafting, targeting, and distribution to have the desired impact. Effective media communication depends on understanding the target audience, choosing the appropriate media channel, and creating well-crafted messages that resonate with the audience. With these skills, individuals and organizations can harness the power of media communication to bring about social change, raise awareness, and motivate action.

CHAPTER 14: PUBLIC SPEAKING SKILLS

Public speaking is one of the most common fears people face, but it is also an essential skill in many areas of life. From giving presentations at work to delivering speeches at weddings or other events, it is important to be able to communicate effectively in front of an audience. In this chapter, we will explore the importance of public speaking, strategies for overcoming public speaking anxiety, and techniques for delivering engaging speeches.

The Importance of Public Speaking

Public speaking is an important skill in many areas of life. At work, you may need to deliver presentations to managers, colleagues, or clients to demonstrate your ideas, plans or projects. In school or college, you may be asked to give presentations or speeches as part of your coursework. In social situations, you may need to give a speech at a wedding or other event to express your gratitude or admiration for someone. Being able to speak confidently and clearly in front of an audience is an essential skill for success.

Overcoming Public Speaking Anxiety

For many people, the thought of standing in front of an audience and speaking is terrifying. They may experience physical symptoms such as sweating or shaking, or the fear may be so strong that they refuse to speak in public at all. However, there are strategies that can help you overcome public speaking anxiety.

One approach is to practice relaxation techniques, such as deep breathing or meditation. These techniques can help you calm your nerves and feel more comfortable before and during a speech. Another approach is to visualize success. Before the speech, imagine yourself giving a successful speech and receiving positive feedback from the audience. This can help build confidence and reduce anxiety.

Preparing for a Speech

Preparing a speech is an important step in ensuring that you deliver an engaging presentation. The first step is to determine your purpose and message. What do you want to communicate with your audience? What is the key takeaway you want your listeners to remember?

Once you have determined your purpose and message, it is important to research your topic thoroughly. You should gather data, statistics, and other supporting information that will reinforce your message. This can also help you anticipate questions from the audience.

Organizing Your Speech

A well-organized speech is key to keeping your audience engaged and conveying your message effectively. An effective organization starts with an introduction that grabs the audience's attention and provides an overview of what you will be discussing. Then, you move to the main body of the speech, where you will present your data and supporting information in an organized, logical manner. Finally, you will conclude your speech by summarizing your main points and leaving your audience with a memorable ending statement.

Captivating Your Audience

Keeping your audience engaged during your speech is crucial. There are several techniques you can use to do this. One is to use stories or anecdotes to illustrate your points. This can help make your message more relatable and memorable for your audience. Another technique is to use humor when appropriate. Humor can help to break the ice with your audience and make them feel more comfortable.

Using Visual Aids Effectively

Visual aids, such as slideshows or handouts, can be a useful tool for supporting your message and keeping your audience engaged. However, it is important to use visual aids effectively. They should be simple, visually appealing, and easy to read. Avoid using too much visual information that can distract your audience from your message.

Handling Questions and Feedback

During the speech, it is likely that your audience will have questions or comments. It is important to be prepared for this and have a plan for handling questions and feedback. You can ask audience members to hold their questions until the end of the speech or encourage them to ask questions throughout. It is also important to be prepared to respond to feedback or criticism, keeping in mind that it should be constructive and used to help you improve in the future.

Delivering Engaging Speeches

Delivering a memorable speech requires more than just technique and preparation. You also need to engage your audience on an emotional level. One way to do this is to use stories or examples that will resonate with your audience. You can also use rhetorical techniques, such as repetition or parallelism, to emphasize important points. Finally, remember to speak with confidence and enthusiasm to show your audience that you believe in your message.

In conclusion, public speaking is an important skill that can help you succeed in many areas of life. While it is natural to feel nervous or anxious, there are strategies that can help you overcome these fears and deliver engaging speeches. By preparing thoroughly, organizing your message effectively, and engaging your audience on an emotional level, you can become a confident and effective public speaker.

CHAPTER 15: EFFECTIVE COMMUNICATION IN ROMANTIC RELATIONSHIPS

Effective communication is essential for any kind of relationship, but it is especially crucial for romantic relationships. True intimacy can only be achieved through open and honest communication. Communication establishes trust, understanding, and connection. However, despite its importance, communication in romantic relationships can be challenging. Misunderstandings, hurt feelings, and disagreements are common. Here are some tips for effective communication in romantic relationships:

1. Establish clear communication goals

Before beginning any conversation, it is important to establish clear communication goals. What do you hope to achieve through talking with your partner? How do you want your partner to feel after the conversation? Setting clear goals will help keep the conversation on track and prevent misunderstandings.

2. Listen actively

Active listening is an important skill in any relationship, but it is particularly important in romantic relationships. Active listening means fully focusing on your partner and trying to understand their perspective. Avoid interrupting, and ask clarifying questions to ensure that you fully understand what your partner is saying.

3. Communicate love and affection

It is important to communicate love and affection to your partner regularly. Small gestures, such as compliments or acts of kindness, can go a long way in strengthening your relationship. In addition, verbalizing your affection can help your partner feel loved and appreciated.

4. Handle conflicts respectfully

No relationship is without its conflicts. However, it is important to handle conflicts respectfully. Avoid attacking your partner or using hurtful language. Instead, focus on the issues at hand and work together to find solutions. It is important to remember that conflicts are an opportunity for growth and better understanding.

5. Communication strategies for long-distance relationships

Communication can be especially challenging in long-distance relationships. It is important to establish regular communication routines, such as scheduled phone calls or virtual dates. In addition, it can be helpful to use technology to stay connected, such as sending messages or photos throughout the day. Communication is key to maintaining a strong connection, even from a distance.

6. Managing jealousy and trust issues

Jealousy and trust issues are common in romantic relationships. However, they can be particularly damaging if not managed effectively. Open and honest communication is important when dealing with jealousy or trust issues. Be sure to communicate your feelings without blaming your partner. It is also important to establish clear boundaries and work together to build trust.

7. Improving sexual communication

Open communication is vital to a healthy sexual relationship. It is important to communicate your needs and desires to your partner, as well as listening to theirs. Be open to exploring new ideas and techniques. Sexual communication can be vulnerable, but it is an essential component of a healthy relationship.

8. Maintaining healthy relationships

Finally, maintaining a healthy relationship requires ongoing communication. Regular check-ins, such as weekly or monthly conversations, can help ensure that both partners are on the same page. Remember that relationships require effort and communication. It is important to prioritize your relationship and make time for communication and connection.

CHAPTER 16: EFFECTIVE COMMUNICATION IN FRIENDSHIP

Friendship is one of the most cherished aspects of our lives. It is the bond that we share with individuals who are not our family members but are equally important. Effective communication is a cornerstone of any healthy and meaningful friendship. In this chapter, we will explore the importance of effective communication in friendships, how to build trust and loyalty, and how to handle conflicts and changes within the friendship.

The Importance of Communication in Friendships

The foundation of any successful friendship is communication. When you communicate openly, honestly, and effectively with your friends, you build a bond that can withstand any obstacle. Communication in friendships takes on many forms, including verbal, non-verbal, and written communication. Effective communication skills can help strengthen and maintain the bond between friends.

Communicating Emotions and Feelings

One of the most critical elements of effective communication in friendships is the ability to express emotions and feelings freely. It is essential to share your thoughts, feelings, and concerns with your friends to develop trust, intimacy, and mutual understanding. It may take time and effort to reach a level of comfort in expressing your emotions and feelings, but it is worth the investment.

Building Trust and Loyalty

Trust is the cornerstone of any healthy friendship. It develops over time through open, honest, and consistent communication. When you communicate effectively with your friends, you build a sense of trust and loyalty that strengthens the bond. It is crucial to follow through on your commitments and be honest about your thoughts, feelings, and intentions. Trust and loyalty can take years to build but can be lost in an instant.

Handling Conflicts in Friendships

Conflicts are unavoidable in any relationship, including friendships. It is essential to deal with conflicts constructively to prevent long-term damage to the friendship. Effective communication skills can help you navigate conflicts successfully. Keep your cool, speak calmly and respectfully, and listen actively to your friend's perspective. Be willing to compromise, if necessary, to reach a solution that satisfies both parties.

Communication in Group Friendships

Group friendships can be complex, with different personalities, perspectives, and opinions. It is important to communicate effectively within the group to foster a positive dynamic. Take the time to listen actively to each group member's thoughts, feelings, and concerns. Honor each member's unique perspective, and be open-minded to their suggestions. Effective communication skills can help the group work together to achieve a common goal.

Navigating Changes in Friendships

Friendships go through changes over time. Individuals may change, move or go through life changes that affect the friendship. It is important to communicate openly and honestly during these changes to maintain the friendship's bond. Effective communication skills can help you adapt to the changes while still maintaining the friendship.

Maintaining Strong and Healthy Friendships

Maintaining strong and healthy friendships requires effort and investment. Consistent communication builds trust, loyalty, and mutual understanding. It is essential to make time for your friends and follow through on your commitments. Celebrate your friends' victories and be there for them during tough times. Remember the small things, like sending a quick text, checking in on them, or sending a gift on their special day.

Being a Good Friend

Being a good friend requires effective communication skills, as communication is the foundation of any healthy friendship. To be a good friend, you must be willing to listen, understand, and respect your friends' thoughts, feelings, and perspectives. Show empathy, offer support, and be there for your friends when they need you. Be honest, remain confidential, and honor your commitments. Being a good friend takes effort and investment but is worth the reward of an enduring friendship.

Conclusion

Effective communication skills are essential in building and maintaining healthy and meaningful friendships. Open, honest, and consistent communication builds trust, loyalty, and mutual understanding. It is essential to communicate emotions and feelings, handle conflicts constructively, and adapt to changing circumstances. Maintaining strong and healthy friendships takes effort and investment but is worth the reward of an enduring bond that can withstand any obstacle.

CHAPTER 17: EFFECTIVE COMMUNICATION AT WORK

Effective communication is fundamental for success in any workplace. It allows colleagues to work together efficiently, share ideas and provide innovative solutions. Communication is an essential tool for achieving goals, measuring progress and avoiding misunderstandings. Moreover, effective communication also helps to build positive relationships, increase job satisfaction and reduce workplace stress.

Communication with Colleagues and Supervisors

Establishing open and honest communication with colleagues and supervisors is key to building a productive and healthy workplace. The ability to communicate effectively allows individuals to share their thoughts and ideas with others and work toward common goals. Requesting input from colleagues on projects, providing feedback and expressing gratitude are basic forms of effective communication.

Nonverbal communication, such as facial expressions and body language, can also play a critical role in communication with colleagues. Conveying acknowledgement and respect through eye contact and active listening can foster healthy workplace relationships.

Business Writing and Email Etiquette

Effective written communication skills are imperative in the modern-day workplace, where written exchanges, particularly email, are the primary means of communication. Clear and concise emails allow recipients to quickly understand the purpose of the communication and respond accordingly. Additionally, well-written business writing, such as reports and proposals, can persuade and influence decisions.

Email etiquette involves the use of clear and professional language as well as structure. Emails should aim to convey information effectively while keeping communication respectful and courteous.

Listening Skills in the Workplace

Active listening skills are crucial in the workplace as it demonstrates to colleagues and supervisors that their contributions are valuable. Active listening involves full concentration, attention to nonverbal cues and acknowledging the message by providing feedback.

Giving and Receiving Feedback

Feedback is an essential component of improvement and should be delivered courteously, constructively and with an aim to reject any notions of negativity to the recipient. Providing positive feedback is important to celebrate success and inspire future successes. Similarly, constructive feedback that is delivered with respect can provide valuable insight to enhance performance. Receiving feedback with an open mind and a positive attitude compounds the effectiveness of organizational feedback system designs.

Conflict Resolution Techniques

Conflicts are an inevitable part of the workplace. However, how an individual deals with conflicts determines how well they can communicate with colleagues and supervisors. When conflicts arise, an approach using empathy and diplomacy, actively seeking common goals and listening to all sides, leaves all parties feeling valued and decreases the likelihood of future conflicts arising.

Workplace Communication Technologies

Workplace communication technologies have changed dramatically in recent years. Emails, Skype, and video conferencing have become commonplace with revolutionized personalization and mobility. Also, technology has allowed for documents to be digitized and stored easily, making them accessible to everyone, everywhere, all the time.

Improving Team Communication

Team communication involves sharing information with team members, discussing goals and providing feedback. Improving team communication requires open and real conversations with team members, gathering inputs and making each member feel like their opinions matter. Finally, organizations could also benefit from communication surveys to evaluate the level of organization-wide communication.

In Summary

Effective workplace communication relies on the ability of workers to establish and maintain effective communication with colleagues and supervisors. Effective communication skills, such as email etiquette, active listening, feedback delivery, conflict resolution techniques, and the use of communication technologies support the maintenance of healthy work relationships and increase job satisfaction.

CHAPTER 18: EFFECTIVE COMMUNICATION IN DATING AND COURTSHIP

When it comes to dating and courtship, effective communication is crucial for building a strong and healthy relationship. The way we communicate with our romantic partners can make or break a relationship, and therefore it is essential to understand how to communicate effectively in a romantic context.

Building Attraction Through Communication

Effective communication is a powerful tool for building attraction and intimacy in a relationship. When we communicate effectively with our partner, we show them that we are interested in them, and we value their thoughts and feelings. Good communication skills make us more attractive to our partner, and it helps to build trust and emotional connections.

Understanding the Other Person's Communication Style

To communicate effectively, it is important to understand our partner's communication style. Every person has a unique way of communicating, and it is essential to be aware of our partner's particular style. This includes taking into account factors such as their cultural background, personality, and communication preferences.

Communicating Expectations and Boundaries

Effective communication in dating and courtship involves communicating our expectations and boundaries clearly. When we communicate our expectations, we are letting our partner know what we want from the relationship and what are our priorities. Similarly, communicating our boundaries helps to establish what we are comfortable with and what our limits are. When we communicate these things effectively, it helps to prevent misunderstandings and provides a clear framework for the relationship.

Handling Conflicts in Relationships

Communication plays a crucial role in resolving conflicts in romantic relationships. Conflicts are inevitable in any relationship, and how we handle those conflicts can determine the success or failure of the relationship. When communicating during conflicts, it is essential to remain respectful and attentive to our partner's needs. Active listening and empathy can help us to understand the perspective of our partner and work towards a resolution that is acceptable to both parties.

Improving Sexual Communication

Sexual communication is an essential aspect of romantic relationships but can often be a challenging topic to discuss. Effective communication in this area involves being open and honest about our sexual desires and preferences. It is also important to be respectful of our partner's boundaries and to communicate our own boundaries clearly. Good communication between partners can help to build trust in this area and can lead to a more fulfilling sexual relationship.

Communication in Long-Term Relationships

Effective communication is essential for building and maintaining long-term relationships. As relationships progress, communication styles may change, and it is important to adapt to these changes. It is crucial to continue to communicate expectations and boundaries, and to remain open and honest with our partner. Effective communication also involves finding ways to work together and overcome challenges that may arise.

Building Strong, Healthy Relationships

All relationships require effort and commitment to succeed. Effective communication is a fundamental aspect of building strong, healthy relationships. It helps to build trust, intimacy, and emotional connections between partners. Effective communication involves being open, honest, and respectful in all aspects of our relationship. It involves being attentive to our partner's needs and making an effort to understand their perspective.

In conclusion, effective communication is essential for building and maintaining healthy, fulfilling romantic relationships. It helps to build attraction and intimacy, establish expectations and boundaries, handle conflicts, improve sexual communication, and build strong relationships over the long term. By being attentive, empathetic, and communicative with our romantic partners, we can build lasting relationships that are built on trust, respect, and mutual understanding.

CHAPTER 19: EFFECTIVE COMMUNICATION IN PARENTING

Parenting is one of the most important and rewarding roles in life. It also comes with its fair share of challenges, and communication is key to successfully navigating them. Effective communication in parenting involves not just talking to your children, but also actively listening, understanding, and responding to their needs. In this chapter, we will explore the importance of effective communication in parenting and provide strategies for nurturing healthy family communication.

Communicating with Children of Different Ages

Effective communication with children requires understanding their developmental stages. The way we communicate with a toddler is very different from how we communicate with a teenager. Young children typically have a shorter attention span and limited vocabulary, so it's important to use simple and concise language when communicating with them. For example, use short sentences and repetition to reinforce important messages. Make eye contact and use gestures and facial expressions to help them understand the message.

Older children and teenagers have a more developed vocabulary and can understand more complex language. It's important to listen to them and involve them in conversations. Encourage them to express their thoughts and feelings, and respond with empathy and understanding. Avoid negative criticism or judgment, instead provide clear explanations and reasoning for rules and restrictions.

Building Positive Relationships with Children

Positive reinforcement is a powerful tool in building good communication with children. Children respond well to praise, encouragement, and positive feedback. When they know they are appreciated, they feel valued and respected. On the other hand, negative reinforcement such as punishment or yelling can damage the parent-child relationship and lead to poor communication. When they feel emotionally safe and secure, they are more likely to open up and share their thoughts and feelings with you.

Providing Guidance and Discipline

Guidance and discipline are essential components of parenting, but they require effective communication. In order to guide children, parents must first understand their perspectives and feelings. Encourage children to express their thoughts and feelings without fear or hesitation. When children feel heard, they are more likely to accept guidance and discipline.

When it comes to discipline, it is important to be clear and consistent with the expectations, rules, and consequences. Providing reasonable consequences and identifying an alternative behavior to practice for future correction is an effective discipline technique. In addition, discipline should be done in the right time and place, and take place within the structure of a supportive family environment.

Handling Conflicts in Families

Conflict is inevitable in any family, and it is important for parents to handle it effectively. Healthy communication during conflicts requires active listening, clear and honest communication, and empathy. Allow everyone to share their feelings and thoughts, and encourage cooperation in problem-solving by talking through the issue. Restate your understanding of the conflict and discuss acceptable compromise, considering the perspective of all parties involved. Moving forward with a plan of action requires mutual acceptance and commitment to growth.

Parental Communication Styles

Parents often have different communication styles that can lead to conflicts. For example, one parent may be more authoritarian while the other may be more permissive. Effective parenting communication requires compromise and collaboration to create an environment that is safe, supportive, and nurturing for the needs of the child.

Parenting Challenges and Solutions

Effective communication is often the solution to many common parenting challenges. With effective communication, parents can work together to solve challenging situations such as those with a child's behavior, managing stress and anxiety, or balancing work and family time. A problem-solving approach that's collaborative, empathic and supportive will cultivate healthy family dynamics and relationship.

Nurturing Healthy Family Communication

Nurturing healthy family communication involves positive reinforcement, mutual respect, and effective communication skills. Encourage regular family meetings to discuss important issues and upcoming events, express appreciation for one another, clarify goals and expectations, and encourage positive communication skills. Establishing open, honest lines of communication will ensure healthy family relationships and positive growth. Practice self-reflection and continue to improve listening skills, adjust communication styles, and express gratitude for the opportunity and responsibility of parenting.

Conclusion

Effective communication in parenting is essential for creating meaningful and healthy relationships with our children. By understanding their developmental stages and communication needs, we can build positive relationships and provide guidance and discipline. Handling conflicts and challenges require active listening, compromise, and empathy. Nurture healthy family communication through a collaborative and supportive approach and maintain lasting relationships with those we love.

CHAPTER 20: EFFECTIVE COMMUNICATION IN SPIRITUAL AND RELIGIOUS SETTINGS

For many people, spiritual and religious beliefs are an essential part of their lives. Whether they practice in a house of worship, attend spiritual retreats or practice mindfulness, effective communication is key to creating deeper and more meaningful relationships with others and the divine.

In this chapter, we will explore the importance of effective communication in spiritual and religious settings, and techniques for enhancing communication skills.

Communicating with Diverse Communities

Effective communication in spiritual or religious settings means being aware and respectful of diversity. This may include differences in language, race, ethnicity, or culture. To communicate effectively, it's essential to understand the cultural norms and practices of diverse communities.

Listening and Empathy in Spiritual Communication

Effective communication in spiritual settings is not just about speaking; it's also about listening. Listening skills are essential to effective communication in spiritual settings, where people often need someone to listen to them. It requires empathy, the ability to feel what another person is feeling, and understand their perspectives.

Handling Conflicts and Disagreements

Conflicts and disagreements are inevitable. Still, understanding how to handle them positively and respectfully is essential in spiritual and religious settings. These may involve dealing with religious or spiritual beliefs that conflict with one another, disputes over leadership or community direction, or disagreements over rituals and practices. Understanding conflict resolution techniques, such as active listening, collaboration, and mediation, can be crucial to resolving disagreements.

Communication in Rituals and Ceremonies

Rituals and ceremonies are essential in many religious and spiritual traditions. Communication during these events varies, and it is important to understand how to communicate in a way that respects the significance of the ritual. This may include knowing appropriate rituals and behaviors, choosing relevant language, respecting privacy, and confidentiality.

Building Spiritual Community Through Communication

Building spiritual communities means cultivating deep connections and relationships with each other. Effective communication is vital to building these relationships. Communication builds connections by sharing experiences and emotions, supporting one another in times of need, and working together towards a common goal.

Exploring Deeper Spiritual and Religious Questions

Effective communication in spiritual and religious settings can help explore complicated topics and address complex questions. It is important to create a safe space where people feel comfortable sharing their beliefs and perspectives without judgment or fear.

Communicating and Connecting with the Divine

Ultimately, effective communication in spiritual and religious settings is about connecting with the divine. Whether praying, meditating, or reflecting, the act of communication is one means of establishing that connection. This means creating an environment that supports spiritual and religious practices, and communication that encourages a sense of connection and purpose.

Conclusion

Effective communication skills are essential in spiritual and religious settings. Whether it is listening empathetically, handling conflicts respectfully, building deeper connections with others, or exploring challenging spiritual questions, effective communication allows people to connect with one another and the divine. It is the key to meaningful and transformative spiritual experiences that last a lifetime.

Remember that communication is a two-way process, and it requires effort from both parties involved. You can't expect others to understand you if you don't make an effort to communicate effectively. Practice makes perfect when it comes to communication skills, so keep working on them every day.

With time and practice, you will become better at expressing yourself clearly and understanding the needs of others. Effective communication can help you build lasting relationships, achieve your goals in life and career, and avoid misunderstandings that could lead to conflict.

I hope this book has been helpful in giving you valuable insights into how to communicate more effectively with those around you. Remember that effective communication takes practice but is worth the effort!

ABOUT THE AUTHOR

Ray Goodwin

Ray Goodwin, is the author behind this series of captivating books on Business Development and self improvement, and has left an indelible mark on the field. He was born and raised in the bustling city of London, where he developed a strong work ethic and an insatiable curiosity about the inner workings of successful businesses. Throughout his illustrious career, Ray leveraged his extensive knowledge and experience to help numerous companies flourish and prosper.

His keen insights and innovative strategies has earned him recognition, driving him to share his expertise with others. Ray believes in the power of sharing knowledge to elevate businesses and empower aspiring entrepreneurs.

Ray's dedication to his craft is evident in the numerous books he has authored on business development and self improvement. His writing style seamlessly blends practical advice, thought-provoking concepts, and real-life case studies, making his books invaluable resources for business professionals and novices alike. His ability to distill complex concepts into accessible language has greatly impacted the lives and careers of countless individuals.

Now retired from the corporate world, Ray and his beloved wife have settled in the idyllic English countryside. Surrounded by the beauty of nature, Ray finds inspiration for his writing and indulges in his hobbies.

Ray Goodwin's books continue to serve as enduring guides for those seeking success in the business world. With a wealth of experience and a deep understanding of the inner workings of businesses, Ray's work remains a testament to his passion for sharing knowledge and helping others flourish.